the Void

Exploring
the Mind

Exploring the Void

A Lent Course

NICHOLAS and JUDITH CALVER

DARTON · LONGMAN + TODD

First published in 2008 by
Darton, Longman and Todd Ltd
1 Spencer Court
140–142 Wandsworth High Street
London SW18 4JJ

ISBN-10: 0–232–52751–2
ISBN-13: 978–0–232–52751–3

A catalogue record for this book is available
from the British Library.

This publication has not been authorised by Film 4 or
the UK Film Council.

Designed and produced by Sandie Boccacci
Set in 9.5/12pt Palatino
Printed and bound in Great Britain by
Athenaeum Press, Gateshead, Tyne and Wear

*To all the people in St John's, Redhill
who made the journey*

*and to Rachel, Sarah, Chris and Hannah
who had to live it.*

This course began as a series of sessions on the film *Touching the Void* with the Salt and Pepper group at St John the Evangelist, Redhill, Surrey – a group of young people aged 13 to 16. These sessions were then developed into a Lent course which was followed by a number of groups in the church in 2006. We are grateful to many people for their support and input along the way, including: Phyllida Dallman who was a travelling companion in the Salt and Pepper sessions; all the leaders and members of the Lent groups; and all those who read and commented on this text. Above all, we are grateful to Joe Simpson and Simon Yates for their inspiration in book and film.

Contents

Contents

Introduction

'Climb every mountain … till you find your dream.' The oft-sung advice from the Mother Superior in *The Sound of Music* belies the gritty determination of mountaineers set on pushing back the boundaries and grappling with all that the forces of nature throw at them.

In 1985 two young mountaineers, Joe Simpson and Simon Yates, set out to climb Siula Grande in Peru, another in a long string of climbs they had undertaken around the world. Spurred on by their ambition to be the first to climb its west face, they set out alone to climb it 'Alpine style' – in a single push with just a rucksack of equipment. Their only supporter was a young traveller they had met on their way.

This Lent course uses extracts from the film *Touching the Void*, based on Joe's book of the same name, which portrays the dramatic events of that climb and descent. Directed by Kevin MacDonald, it won the Alexander Korda Award for Best British Film at the 2004 BAFTA Awards and sparked intense interest in the events on that mountainside and the characters' battle for survival.

In the film Joe and Simon comment on the story as it unfolds and recall their thoughts and feelings at the time. Both were experienced climbers. Joe is honest about what first motivated him as a young, eager climber:

> I wanted to be a great climber, craved the false glory that I thought went with being a 'hard man'. I did not realise then that I could never be something that existed only in my boastful mind. At the same time, it seemed wrong to want such things, shallow and superficial. I suppose it was only ambition, vaunting ambition perhaps, a goal which gave me incentive, but which to my guilt-ridden lapsed Catholic mind was wrong. Pride was a sin. So I persuaded myself I climbed because the routes were good, so aesthetically beautiful, and so fine, which was partly true as well as being an easy way out.[1]

Perhaps it was this very ambition which led Joe to mountain tops around the world and sustained his grip on life on the Siula Grande.

Simon is also honest about what lures him to these new challenges:

> For me, travelling to an unknown place to
> ascend an unclimbed mountain provides the
> challenge, risk and uncertainty that I consider
> are the true ingredients of a true adventure.[2]

The third character we meet is Richard Hawking, a
young man who was travelling around South America
and agreed to mind the climbers' equipment while
they were on the peak. He knew nothing about
mountaineering and so little about Simon and Joe that
he didn't even know their surnames. And yet, as we
find out, he plays his own part in the events that
unfold.

Three different characters, thrown into the same
story. The same will be true of groups following this
course. Some members will know each other well,
others will be strangers when they embark on the
journey. But all will be trusting each other with their
life stories as they journey together.

It is an important aspect of this course that it does
not seek to debate the possible rights or wrongs of the
characters' actions on the mountain, nor to decide
whether their reflections and motivations are 'right' or
'wrong'. Rather, it uses scenes from the film to trigger
thoughts and discussion on our own journeying –
even though, for most of us, the peaks and troughs of
our life stories are far less extreme than those experienced in the Peruvian mountains. And anyway, how
can we choose to apportion blame or forgiveness for

events which are so far from our own experience? In *Engleby* by Sebastian Faulks, a character begs of the reader:

> Please, whatever you do, don't 'forgive' me.
> Don't ask for 'closure' or 'release' for me because
> it's not really me you'd be asking for, but your-
> selves: granting me forgiveness would free you
> from your own anguish at what I did; it would
> be a way of putting me out of your mind.[3]

And while the characters' actions are not for our criticism, nor are their beliefs. Joe discovers in the film that, despite a Catholic upbringing and despite being in a desperate situation, he has no inclination to call on God for help. This revelation in the film resulted in bags of post from those who hoped to persuade him that he was 'wrong'. On his website he writes:

> I would say that I am a well-educated, widely
> read, extensively travelled, reasonably articulate
> and philosophically and emotionally sensitive
> individual. That I am an Atheist was a difficult
> and long pondered decision. That my lack of
> belief was tested in a crucible far more testing
> than most other people have experienced should
> at very least give me the right to quietly state my
> beliefs when asked and not be plagued by people
> who think I am wrong and they are right.[4]

The very fact that most people will be following this course during Lent, and as they prepare for Easter, suggests that they are likely to be exploring a different faith path from Joe's. However, respect for co-travellers is vital. Group members will have come to their opinions and beliefs by virtue of the differing paths they have followed on their journey through life thus far. All their stories are valid and valuable to the group.

Similarly, all group members will have different motivations for embarking on this journey together. Simon writes:

> Many of us plan the same long-term adventure; to find a partner, to make a home and to raise children. We can almost take this for granted, as if it is a certainty. Those that aspire to things outside of this norm are often considered eccentric, strange or weird, while those who want to pursue the peaks of mountains, the bottoms of oceans or the depths of caves, and are willing to risk their lives to do so, are sometimes considered totally mad. Yet whether we court risks or not, nothing is certain.[5]

We may not share Simon and Joe's steely ambition to scale unconquered peaks, but like them, we can dare to follow our dreams.

George Mallory, who was later to perish on Mount

Everest, wrote in his journal after reaching the summit of Mont Blanc in 1911:

> One must conquer, achieve, get to the top; one must know the end to be convinced that one can win the end – to know there's no dream that mustn't be dared.

His words resonated with Joe who, reflecting on another climb in his career, comments:

> Mallory wholeheartedly believed there was no dream that must not be dared; his life stretched to the very end. Perhaps, like him, we have no choice but to go back and dare our dreams. We had looked up at the vastness of the Eiger filled with a mixture of exultation and apprehension about what we were about to do in the morning. To me that is everything mountain climbing is about – the outcome uncertain, the spirit sub-dued, the challenge open – a free choice to take up or walk away from. More than anything it is about taking part – not success or failure, simply being there and making the choice.[6]

Perhaps the Mother Superior had it right all along:

> Climb every mountain, search high and low,
> Follow every byway, every path you know.

Climb every mountain, ford every stream,
Follow every rainbow, till you find your dream –
A dream that will need all the love you can give
Every day of your life, for as long as you live.[7]

Week One:

Travelling Companions

On the Ascent

According to the Acts of the Apostles, Christians were first known as followers of 'The Way', and many Christian writers have used the image of a journey as a means of understanding the Christian life. Perhaps the best-known work is John Bunyan's spiritual classic *Pilgrim's Progress*, written towards the end of the seventeenth century. Its full title, *The pilgrim's progress from this world to that which is to come*, gives a clue to the fact that Bunyan placed rather more emphasis on the destination than the journey.

Looking to Christian art rather than literature, you might be familiar with the paintings of *The Broad and Narrow Way*, nineteenth-century depictions of Jesus' words in Matthew's Gospel about entering through the narrow gate rather than the wide one (Matt. 7:13–14).[1] To the left, signposted 'Death and Damnation', is a wide gateway with a large 'Welcome' sign above it, leading to a path on which many are travelling. However, at the top of the hill and unbeknown to them, the way leads to death and destruction and the flames of hellfire. To the right, signposted 'Life and Salvation', there is a small doorway, half

hidden in a wall, and from it leads a steep and narrow
path, bordered by a church and a Calvary, on which
far fewer people are travelling, and at the end of
which lies the heavenly city.

Both this image and *Pilgrim's Progress* give the
impression that life is more about the destination – our
journey through life is simply a means to an end, and
that end is heaven if you follow the narrow way, or
hell if you get it wrong and follow the broad way.

But there is another way of understanding life. You
may have heard the saying, 'Life is a journey, not a
destination'. If we look at life in this way, it is not
where we are heading that is important but what
happens to us along the way. Life, especially the
Christian life, is a journey of self-discovery in
response to the call of Christ. The first disciples
embarked on that journey and he still calls us today.
The journey may not take us as far away as Peru or up
steep mountains, but the real journey we make is an
inward and spiritual one, through which our experiences of life help us grow into the people we are
meant to be.

The early Church Fathers – the formulators of
Christian doctrine in the first few centuries following
the New Testament period – often use the phrase,
'God became man, that we might become God'. It is a
good way of expressing the idea that our journey is a
process of God-given growth and change.

Lent, and particularly the last week of Lent, is

about entering into that journey – one that we share with Christ. Lent courses, such as this one, tend to run for five weeks, leaving the last week of Lent free for the special services of Holy Week. What happens in churches during Holy Week can vary tremendously according to their tradition, but in most churches there will be some services and events that are rather different from the usual.

In many areas there is a Procession of Witness on Good Friday in which people from different churches take part in a walk together, following a cross carried at the front of the procession. Taking part in something like this can be a powerful and moving experience, even if sometimes it first means that we have to face our own embarrassment and awkwardness at the looks we may receive from passers by. But such feelings help us to identify in a small way with how Jesus may have felt as he made his final journey through the streets of Jerusalem.

This course is about helping us to see that our journey is also Jesus' journey and that his journey is also ours. It follows a film about a real-life journey that two climbers – Simon Yates and Joe Simpson – made, accompanied by Richard Hawking, someone they bumped into on the way. Their journey, although its outward focus was the ascent – and descent – of Peru's Siula Grande, was also for each of them an inward journey that challenged and changed them in a number of ways.

As a follower of this course you too are embarking on a journey. Though your outward journey may never involve climbing a Peruvian mountain, your inner journey may, at times in your life, follow a similar path to that of those three climbers. Your fellow travellers will be not only your fellow course participants but also all those with whom you come into contact outside the sessions as you go about your daily routine, and maybe people from your past as well.

Above all, what matters is not getting to the end but how you get there. Remember that this course is a journey, not a destination.

Happy travelling!

Session 1

○ **Introduction**   **(10–15 min.)**
Give each person a chance to introduce themselves, including whether they have attended a Lent course before. If so, how did they find it? Or, if this is the first one they have attended, how do they feel about it?

◀ **DVD**   **(7 min.)**
From the Film 4 logo (00.07) to just after when Joe says, 'Christ, it's big. Looks harder than I thought, expected. But I was excited' (06.46).

🐘 **Discuss** (5 min.)

Think about what Joe and Simon embarked upon. How does what they did make you feel?

📖 **Read** (3 min.)

Joe: 'We climbed because it's fun … and it was fun – it was brilliant fun – and every now and then it went wildly wrong and then it wasn't.'

Simon: 'To climb mountains that have not been climbed before, or a new route to a mountain, is what my climbing life had been moving towards … There's a great unknown there. What's so compelling is stepping into that unknown.'

Luke 5:1–11: Jesus calls the first disciples.

🐘 **Discuss** (5–10 min.)

Sports psychologists say that athletes are primarily motivated either by the hope of success or the fear of failure. What do you feel motivates you? Has your motivation varied at different stages of your journey through life?

📖 **Read** (1 min.)

Luke 9:57–62: The cost of following Jesus.

🗨 Ponder   **(1 min.)**

Alpine climbing is a very committed way of climbing. You have no line of retreat.

Have there been times in your life when burning bridges has enabled you to move on in some way?

🗨 Share   **(5–10 min.)**

Share your thoughts with the group, or keep them to yourself if you'd rather.

◀ DVD   **(8 min.)**

From the end of the last clip (06.46) to '… it was going to go tits up, so we dug a snow cave' (14.00).

📖 Read   **(1 min.)**

Joe: 'The fact that you are tied to your partner means that you put an immense amount of trust in someone else's skill and ability. But at some point you might be thinking, "For God's sake, Simon, don't fall here." The rope can be something that, rather than save your life, can kill you. If you're going to do that sort of climbing, at some point you are going to have to rely wholly on your partner.'

∞ **Personal reflection**   **(5 min.)**
Think about different areas of your life – home, work, spiritual, social etc. Write down some of the people who have helped or hindered you in your journey.

📖 **Read**   **(1 min.)**
Joe in his book, *Touching the Void*: 'Simon and I had found Richard resting in a sleazy hotel in Lima, halfway through his six-month exploration of South America. His wire-rimmed glasses, neat, practical clothing and bird-like mannerisms hid a dry humour and a wild repertoire of beachcombing reminiscences … He travelled the world between bouts of hard work to raise funds. Usually he journeyed alone to see where chance encounters in alien countries would take him.'[2]

🗩 **Discuss**   **(5 min.)**
Richard was a complete stranger to Joe and Simon. He didn't even know which part of Peru he was in! How did his motivation differ from that of Joe and Simon?

📖 **Read**   **(1 min.)**
Luke 24:13–35: The road to Emmaus.

🗩 **Ponder**   **(1 min.)**
Have you had chance encounters that have changed the direction of your life?

📢 Share **(5 min.)**
Share your thoughts with the group, or keep them to yourself if you'd rather.

📖 Read **(2 min.)**
Mark 10:17–27: The rich young ruler.

↪ Personal reflection **(5 min.)**
Alpine climbing meant having to travel light.

Write down some of the things you might need to jettison in order to travel light in your journey. For example, this might include:

- old hurts and resentments
- assumptions and prejudices
- comfort blankets
- too much busy-ness
- guilt
- undue attachment
- poor self-image
- other people's baggage.[3]

What you write is personal to you and not for discussion.

☼ Closing worship **(5 min.)**
See page 86.

On the Descent

'To climb mountains that have not been climbed
before, or a new route to a mountain, is what my
climbing life has been moving towards …
There's a great unknown there. What's so compelling is stepping into that unknown.'

Unlike Simon Yates, you might not find stepping into
the unknown so compelling – rather, you might find it
a bit daunting or even frightening.

The disciples probably felt like that when Jesus
called them to follow him. It was a massive step into
the unknown for them, as they left their nets and their
boats. There's something inherently risky and maybe
a bit frightening about following Jesus. He challenges
us to let go of all the false securities that will ultimately fail us and to find security in spiritual, rather than
physical, terms. We might be tempted to play it safe
and not take a risk. Following Jesus is not like that, as
the children discover in *The Lion, the Witch and the
Wardrobe* by C. S. Lewis. Stepping through the
wardrobe into the land of Narnia, they meet a beaver,
who takes them to his home. He and Mrs Beaver tell
them about Aslan, the King of Narnia, who can free
the land from the spell of the witch:

'Aslan is a lion – the Lion, the great Lion.'

'Ooh!' said Susan, 'I'd thought he was a man. Is he – quite safe? I shall feel rather nervous about meeting a lion.'

'That you will, dearie, and no mistake,' said Mrs Beaver; 'If there's anyone who can appear before Aslan without their knees knocking, they're either braver than most or else just silly.'

'Then he isn't safe?' said Lucy.

'Safe?' said Mr Beaver, 'Don't you hear what Mrs Beaver tells you? Who said anything about safe? 'Course he isn't safe, but he's good.'[4]

We too might feel rather nervous about Jesus' challenge not to play it safe. We might feel as if he is trying to make it hard for us, or that he doesn't understand us. The rich man probably felt that when he asked Jesus how he might inherit eternal life – only to get the reply that he should give away everything he owned. No wonder his face fell and he went away sad!

But Jesus was not trying to be unkind. We read in Mark's account of this incident that 'Jesus looked at him and loved him' (Mark 10:21) – amazing words! Jesus wasn't a killjoy, trying to make the man miserable or make life difficult for him. He loved him and knew deep down what would make the man happy. The rich man sought happiness and security in his riches – and Jesus knew that this could never make him truly happy.

Jesus will challenge each of us in different ways. For most of us, this will not involve selling everything we have and giving the money to the poor. But this is exactly what some Christians have done. One notable example is that of the early thirteenth-century saint St Francis of Assisi. He was born the son of a rich Italian cloth merchant but gave up his wealthy background and inheritance in order to devote himself to a life of poverty.

It was a life that was happier and richer than his old life could ever have been. And in living in this new way, St Francis learnt the truth that in possessing nothing we in fact own everything. This is the truth at the heart of the Gospel – that in giving we receive and in dying we live:

> O Lord, make me an instrument of Thy Peace;
> Where there is hatred, let me sow love;
> Where there is injury, pardon;
> Where there is discord, harmony;
> Where there is doubt, faith;
> Where there is despair, hope;
> Where there is darkness, light;
> And where there is sorrow, joy.
>
> Oh Divine Master, grant that I may not
> so much seek to be consoled as to console;
> to be understood as to understand;
> to be loved as to love;

for it is in giving that we receive;
it is in pardoning that we are pardoned;
and it is in dying that we are born to Eternal Life.[5]

Week Two:

Plateaux and Summits

On the Ascent

Mountains and hilltops figure at key moments in the Bible and are often seen as places where God is to be found. In the Old Testament two mountains are explicitly seen as sacred and where people go to meet with God.

One is Mount Sinai, the 'mountain of the Lord' (sometimes known as Horeb). We read in the book of Exodus how Moses receives his call from God there (Exod. 3), how he speaks with God there and how God reveals his presence there (Exod. 19; 24). It is on Mount Sinai that the covenant between God and Israel is sealed (Deut. 5:2) and where Elijah hears God speak to him not in the earthquake, wind or fire but in the 'still small voice of calm' (1 Kings 19:1–18).

The other mountain we read about is Mount Zion, known as 'God's holy mountain' and seen by the psalmists as the dwelling-place of God (Pss. 9:11; 48:1–3; 76:2; 132:13). It was on Mount Zion that the city of Jerusalem was built.

In the New Testament Jesus has a conversation about mountains with a Samaritan woman he meets at a well (John 4). It takes place on Mount Gerizim, a holy site in the Samaritan religion. Jesus makes it clear that worship of God is spiritual and not limited to a particular

mountain, whether it be the one they are on or the one
that Jews consider holy, Mount Zion. However, mountains still figure prominently in Jesus' own life and
ministry. He is tempted on a mountain and he fre-
quently seeks the mountains as places of refuge and
prayer. His transfiguration takes place on one, where he
is joined by those two Old Testament mountain
climbers, Moses and Elijah. His earthly ministry ends
with his ascension from the top of the Mount of Olives.

Mountain-top experiences may be high points in
our lives in all sorts of ways, but much of our lives
may be lived at a more mundane level. Whether we
enjoy the more level path or the peak experiences will
probably depend on our temperament. We are all
different. Simon Yates says:

> I feel some people recognise that by putting an
> element of danger, uncertainty and challenge
> into their lives, they regain a feeling of freedom
> that they might not have even realised that they
> have lost.[1]

For Simon, climbing mountains and facing the
inevitable dangers and challenges that it presents is
something that he vitally needs – vitally in the very
real sense of necessary for life. But not everyone is the
same, and God is to be found both in the highs and
lows of our lives. Interestingly, the Gospel writers
themselves reflect this fact. You are probably familiar

with the phrase 'The Sermon on the Mount' as a way of describing an episode in Jesus' teaching ministry. But the Sermon on the Mount is only to be found in Matthew (5:1—7:29). Luke has a different version of this episode – the less well-known 'Sermon on the Plain' (Luke 6:17–49).

In Matthew, Jesus *went up* on a mountainside to teach. From there he could look over the top of the crowd and hand down the word from above to those who were beneath him, like Moses who went up the mountain to receive the Ten Commandments. Matthew emphasises Jesus' divinity and places him above the people.

In Luke, however, Jesus went up the mountain not to teach, but to pray. After a night of prayer he chose the 12 disciples. He then, Luke writes, '*came down* with them and stopped at a piece of level ground'. He came down and stood not above the crowd but amongst them, at their level, where people could touch him and he could heal them. In this way Luke emphasises Jesus' humanity and places him among the people.

On the mountain or on the plain, in divinity and in humanity. Both are places where Jesus is to be found, just as we can find him in the ups and downs of our own life experiences. This week's session gives us an opportunity to reflect on what this might mean for us and to hear what it might mean for our fellow travellers.

Session 2

⭢ **Introduction** (5 min.)
Give each person a chance to share any thoughts about the last session or their week.

📖 **Read** (2 min.)
Simon, speaking in last week's clip: 'There's not a lot of risk in our lives normally now. And to put an element of risk back into it takes us out of the humdrum and in that sense it makes you feel more alive.'

Matthew 14:22–31: Peter walks on water.

🗩 **Discuss** (5–10 min.)
Would you have stepped out of the boat? Are you a risk-taker or do you prefer to play it safe?

◀ **DVD** (7 min.)
From where it finished last time (14.00) to 'That night, as we made a brew, the gas ran out' (20.43).

🗩 **Discuss** (5 min.)
How do you think Joe and Simon felt on the summit of Siula Grande?

📖 **Read** **(1 min.)**

Joe: 'I remember thinking, "Oh sod the summit, we've done the face. I can't really be bothered to go all the way up there." And then we thought, "We've come all this way, we might as well stand on the top ..." I don't particularly like summits because 80 per cent of accidents happen on descent.'

↪ **Personal reflection** **(5 min.)**

Draw your life as a line from childhood to now. Have there been ups and downs or has it been more on the level?

💬 **Share** **(10 min.)**

Look at your lifeline. Do you prefer your journey to be on a level plateau or do you like the summit experiences? Share your thoughts with the group, or keep them to yourself if you'd rather.

◀ **DVD** **(17 min.)**

From where it finished last time (20.43) to 'And I would have died pretty soon, actually. The wind chill was very low' (37.26).

📖 **Read** **(2 min.)**

Joe: 'I felt completely helpless and really angry.'

Simon: 'There was nothing I could do. I couldn't get the weight off the rope. I was just there ... My position got more and more desperate.'

Luke 23:32–39: Jesus on the cross.

Discuss   **(5 min.)**
What are your thoughts about Joe and Simon's situations?

Ponder   **(1 min.)**
Has there been a time on your journey when you have felt in a position similar to that of either Joe or Simon?

Share   **(10–15 min.)**
Share your thoughts with the group or keep them to yourself if you'd rather.

☼   **Closing worship**   **(5 min.)**
See page 86.

On the Descent

The journey we make as Christians is one that is made in response to a call. It is a journey that we do not know the destination of, as it is for us a step into the

unknown. The God we worship as Christians is the
one who called Abraham to leave his homeland and to
go on a journey, he knew not where: 'It was by faith
that Abraham obeyed the call to set out for a country
that was the inheritance given to him and his descen-
dants, and that he set out without knowing where he
was going' (Heb. 11:8).

The call of the disciples also had this unknown
quantity about it, not only when they left their nets
but throughout the time they followed Jesus. Peter
had already left his nets and his boat – a massive step
of faith – but Jesus called him to step out again. By
calling him out of the boat, Jesus couldn't have asked
him to do anything that went more against everything
he was familiar with as a fisherman. It was bound up
with his identity, his safety and his security – not just
financial but also psychological. The sides of the boat
were definitely the limits of his comfort zone!

And yet Peter had a sudden recognition that there
was a world beyond the sides of the boat, and that
Jesus was out on the water and not in the boat. He
recognised that this was the moment of decision; he
sensed the implicit call that Jesus' presence evokes. He
checked first – 'Lord, if it is you, tell me to come to you
across the water … Then Peter got out of the boat'
(Matt. 14:28).

Jesus calls us to step out of the safety of our comfort
zone, to take the risk and follow him. Not in a fool-
hardy way – Peter checked first – but in a way that

may well make us feel that we are being asked to do something that scares us – something that makes us fear loss or failure or even appearing the fool. For it is only by taking those risks that we grow into the person we are meant to be. Jesus calls us to leave ourselves in order to become ourselves.

And strangely, sometimes taking the risk is the safest thing to do, and what we perceive as playing it safe is in fact the risky option. Remember the parable of the talents (Luke 19:11-27)? Burying the talent in the ground was not the safe option that it seemed, and what seemed the risky option was in fact the safer one. The risk in playing it safe is the risk that we never grow into the person we are called to be.

> To laugh is to risk appearing the fool.
> To weep is to risk appearing sentimental.
> To reach for another is to risk involvement.
> To expose your ideas, your dreams,
> before a crowd is to risk their loss.
> To love is to risk not being loved in return.
> To live is to risk dying.
> To believe is to risk despair.
> To try is to risk failure.
> But risks must be taken, because the
> greatest hazard in life is to risk nothing.
> The people who risk nothing, do nothing,
> have nothing, are nothing.
> They may avoid suffering and sorrow,

but they cannot learn, feel, change,
grow, love, live.
Chained by their attitudes they are slaves;
they have forfeited their freedom.
Only a person who risks is free.

Author unknown

Week Three:

Breaking Free

On the Ascent

Simon and Joe were joined together. When two people are joined together in marriage, it is sometimes referred to as 'tying the knot'. In the marriage service it is traditional for the priest's stole to be wrapped around the joined hands of the couple like a rope, symbolic of the knot tied between them, and the words of Matthew 19:6 to be proclaimed: 'Those whom God has joined together, let no one put asunder.'[1]

The rope that joined Simon and Joe joined them in a positive, protective way. But the rope always had the potential to work against them. As Joe said in a clip from the first session: 'At some point you might be thinking, "For God's sake, Simon, don't fall here." The rope can be something that, rather than save your life, can kill you.'

For better or for worse, Simon and Joe were joined together and now Joe was aware of the lethal potential contained in the rope that joined them: 'There was nothing I could do. I couldn't get the weight off the rope. I was just there ... My position got more and more desperate.'

The Bible doesn't particularly use the imagery of a
rope as a means of joining things together, but it does
use the imagery of a yoke, and the concept is the same.
In the Old Testament the image of the yoke is used
both in positive terms as an image of obedience to
God (eg Lam. 3:26–27) and in negative terms as an
image of oppression and restraint (eg Lam. 1:14).

In the New Testament Jesus also uses the image of
the yoke, but he only uses it in a positive sense:
'Shoulder my yoke and learn from me, for I am gentle
and humble in heart, and you will find rest for your
souls. Yes, my yoke is easy and my burden light'
(Matt. 11:29–30).

'My yoke is easy.' What does that mean exactly?
The Greek word *chrestos*, translated as 'easy', has a
number of meanings: kind, gentle and helpful. Used
as a description of a yoke, it means that the yoke is
easy to wear, and doesn't chafe or cause discomfort. In
other words, it is a well-fitting yoke.

The yoke that Jesus asks each of us to wear is one
that fits each of us exactly. He doesn't ask us to wear
someone else's yoke; he asks us to wear the yoke that
fits us alone. In other words, following Jesus will be
different for each one of us. He doesn't ask us to
become something we're not in order to follow him –
he challenges us not to burden us but to help us to
grow.

'Shoulder my yoke and *learn from me*,' he says.
Christ wants us to be yoked with him so that we can

learn from him and grow into the person we are truly meant to be. Being yoked to Christ is not something that oppresses us or restricts us. Being yoked to Christ is, paradoxically, the way we are set free – free to be truly ourselves.

The collect for peace and protection in the *Book of Common Prayer* expresses this concept in a wonderful way with the phrase, 'in [God's] service is perfect freedom':

> O God, who art the author of peace and lover of
> concord, in knowledge of whom standeth our
> eternal life, whose service is perfect freedom;
> Defend us thy humble servants in all assaults of
> our enemies; that we, surely trusting in thy
> defence, may not fear the power of any adver-
> saries, through the might of Jesus Christ our
> Lord. Amen.[2]

Session 3

➲ **Introduction** (5 min.)
Give each person a chance to share any thoughts about the last session or their week.

◀ **DVD** (3 min.)
From where it finished last time (37.26) to 'I could

smell the water in the snow around me. I felt that very strongly. It was quite a strange thing' (40.17).

Discuss   **(5–10 min.)**
Would you have cut the rope?

Ponder   **(1 min.)**
Are there situations in your life that you have cut yourself free from or would like to cut yourself free from?

Share   **(10–12 min.)**
Share your thoughts with the group or keep them to yourself if you'd rather.

Read   **(5 min.)**
Mark 12:28–31: Love your neighbour as you love yourself.

Simon, in his book, *Against the Wall*: Some would argue that there was no decision to be made; that cutting the rope and the powerful symbol of trust and friendship it represents should never have entered my mind. Others say that it was simply a matter of survival, something I was forced to do … I knew I had done all that could reasonably be expected of me to save Joe, and now both our lives were being threatened, I had reached a point where I had to look after myself. Although I knew my action might result in his death, I took the decision intuitively in a split second. It simply felt the right thing to do. Ultimately, we all have to look after ourselves, whether on mountains or in day-to-day life. In my view that is not a licence to be selfish, for only by taking good care of ourselves are we able to help others. Away from the mountains, in the complexity of everyday life, the price of neglecting this responsibility might be a marriage breaking down, a disruptive child, a business failing or a house repossessed. In the mountains, the penalty for neglect can often be death.[3]

Discuss (5–10 min.)

'Only by taking good care of ourselves are we able to help others.' What do you think about this?

DVD (8 min.)

From where it finished last time (40.17) to 'I just cried and cried. I thought I'd be tougher than that' (47.46). Note: this extract contains strong language.

Read (1 min.)

Psalm 88:3–5: A cry of despair.

🗨 **Ponder**　　　　　　　　　　　**(1 min.)**
Can you identify with Joe's situation? Have there been times in your life when you have felt that the rope has been cut on you?

🗨 **Share**　　　　　　　　　　　　**(10–12 min.)**
Share your thoughts with the group if you want, or keep them to yourself if you'd rather.

◀ **DVD**　　　　　　　　　　　　　**(2 min.)**
From where it finished last time (47.46) to 'an absolutely enormous crevasse 30 feet wide and just bottomless from where I was looking at it' (49.48).

📖 **Read**　　　　　　　　　　　　**(4 min.)**
Simon: 'By this stage I felt that Joe had been killed the previous day and that now I was going to die as some form of, you know, retribution.'

Simon, in Joe's book, *Touching the Void***:** It gradually lightened. I saw axe marks on the roof, and the night was over. With the coming of the day I thought of what I must do. I knew I wouldn't succeed. It wasn't right for me to succeed. I had thought it all through. This was what must happen to me now. I was no longer afraid, and the dread in the night had gone with the dawn. I knew I would attempt it and I knew it would kill me, but I was going to go through with it. There would be some dignity left to me at least. I had to try my best. It wouldn't be enough, but I would try.

I dressed like a priest before mass, with solemn, careful ceremony. I felt in no hurry to start down and was certain it would be my last day. Filled with a sense of condemnation ... I fastened the last strap of my crampons on to my boot, and then stared silently at my gloved hands. The careful preparation had calmed me. My fear had gone and I was quiet. I felt cold and hard. The night had cleaned me out, purging the guilt and the pain. The loneliness since the cutting had also gone. The thirst had eased. I was as ready as I would ever be.

I smashed the roof of the cave with my axe, and stood up into the blinding glare of a perfect day. I felt watched. Something in the crescent of summits and ridges looked down on me and waited. I stepped from the wreckage of the cave, and started to climb down. I was about to die; I knew it, and they knew it.[4]

🗨 **Ponder** **(1 min.)**
Can you identify with Simon's feelings in any way?

● **Share** **(10–12 min.)**
Share your thoughts with the group or keep them to yourself if you'd rather.

☼ **Closing worship** **(5 min.)**
See page 86.

On the Descent

And then the rope is cut. What was joined together is now divided. Simon writes: 'Some would argue that there was no decision to be made; that cutting the rope and the powerful symbol of trust and friendship it represents should never have entered my mind'[5] – those whom God has joined together let no one put asunder. But he took the decision to cut the rope nonetheless.

It was a selfish decision in one sense, as he had to cut the rope to save himself. But as he says, he felt that 'ultimately, we all have to look after ourselves, for only by taking good care of ourselves are we able to help others.'

Simon was convinced he had killed Joe by his self-ish decision. However, he also intuitively knew that he had made the right decision: 'Although I knew my action might result in his death, I took the decision intuitively in a split second. It simply felt the right thing to do.'

Ironically, cutting that powerful symbol of trust and friendship had not killed Joe; 'I think psychologically I was beaten. 'Cos there was nothing I could do, so I just hung on the rope and waited to die.'

In C. S. Lewis' *The Silver Chair*, Aslan gives two children, Jill Pole and Eustace Scrubb, the task of finding the lost prince of Narnia.[6] They are given four signs they must follow, the last of which was that they would know the lost prince by the fact that he would be the first one to ask them to do something in the name of Aslan.

They journey through Narnia, aided in their quest by their companion, Puddleglum. Eventually, having messed up the first three signs, they arrive at a castle where the wicked Queen and her companion, the Black Knight, live. Every night the Black Knight goes into a frenzy and has to be bound in the Silver Chair from which he must not be released until the frenzy has passed, or else he will turn into a loathsome serpent.

Night comes and the three travellers are alone in the basement, with the Knight bound in his chair. In his frenzy, straining at the ropes that bind him, he begs them to set him free. They cower from him, scared for their lives, but he continues until finally, he begs them, in the name of Aslan, to set him free.

'Oh!' cried the three travellers as though they
had been hurt.

'It's the sign,' said Puddleglum.

'It was the words of the sign,' said Scrubb
more cautiously.

'Oh, what are we to do?' said Jill.

Fearful of the consequences of acting on the sign,
Eustace tried to convince himself it was not really the
sign. How could the sign be on the lips of someone
who wanted to kill them? But Puddleglum knew that
it was the sign:

> 'You see, Aslan didn't tell Pole what would hap-
> pen. He only told her what to do. That fellow
> will be the death of us once he's up, I shouldn't
> wonder. But that doesn't let us off following the
> sign.'

Although he knew their actions might result in their
deaths, like Simon, Puddleglum took the decision intuitively, in a split second. It simply felt the right thing
to do. They cut the ropes, setting the Knight free, and
their action revealed that the Knight was in fact the lost
prince. It was an action that saved both themselves and
the prince.

We should not let fear of the consequences prevent
us from making what we feel to be the right decisions.

Week Four:

Decision
Making

On the Ascent

Decision making is a fundamental part of life, and equally a fundamental part of the spiritual life. To make a decision is to make a choice. The Bible starts with the story of a decision or choice, made first by Eve and then by Adam, to eat the fruit of the tree of the knowledge of good and evil. The consequence of that decision was that they were banished from the garden and the tree of life into a world of sin and death. Deceived by the snake, they chose death rather than life.

A similar decision is presented to the Israelites when they are on the verge of entering the Promised Land, and the importance of making the right choice between death and life is laid before them by God: 'This day I call heaven and earth as witnesses against you that I have set before you life and death, blessings and curses. Now choose life, so that you and your children may live and that you may love the Lord your God, listen to his voice, and hold fast to him' (Deut. 30:19–20).

It is no coincidence that as Jesus enters into his

ministry he, too, is faced with choices. Jesus' public ministry begins with his baptism in which, like us in our own baptisms, he is named and called by God. *Immediately*, as we read in Mark's Gospel, that calling is tested – and 'test' is perhaps a better word than 'temptation'. A test to see what he is made of and see what sort of decisions he will make – decisions about what sort of person he is going to be and in what sort of way he is going to live.

Luke's Gospel gives the clearest picture of the significance of his time of testing. Like Matthew and Mark, Luke tells how Jesus is declared to be God's Son at his baptism. But then, unlike the others, Luke includes a long genealogy tracing Jesus back to 'Adam, the son of God' (Luke 3:21–37), before he goes on to describe Jesus' time of testing in the desert. And at the end of this, the devil tests Jesus' identity. 'If you are the Son of God,' the devil says to him, 'then surely you will be able to do these things. If you can't, then surely you aren't really the Son of God.'

To understand this passage in terms of temptation, which is its traditional interpretation, is to miss the point. It is instead about testing Jesus' identity as the Son of God, and testing it, not only in comparison to Adam, the first son of God, as we have already seen, but also in relation to the people of Israel, who are also seen as the son of God in the Old Testament. In the same way that Jesus is called 'my Son' by God at his baptism, so too Israel is called 'my son' by God (Exod.

4:22f.; Hos. 11:1; Ps. 2:7). When Jesus is being tested by the devil, he quotes from Deuteronomy (6:13; 8:3), and it is in exactly the same passage that we read that God led the people of Israel into the desert: 'These 40 years to humble you and test you in order to see what was in your heart' (Deut. 8:2). But Israel failed the test – the prophets make that quite clear: 'When Israel was a child, I loved him; out of Egypt I called my son, but the more I called Israel, the further they went from me' (Hos. 11:1f.).

Israel's testing in the desert lasts 40 years; Jesus' lasts 40 days. The parallels are clear. Just like Israel, Jesus is being tested to see if he will trust God, worship him alone and not put him to the test. Three sons of God – Adam, Israel and Jesus – and three testings. Adam, son of God, failed his test. Israel, son of God, failed theirs. How will this Son of God fare? He passes the test and so reveals his identity as the true Son of God.[1]

The Church celebrates these 40 days of testing with the season of Lent. For us, Lent is also a time to think about the sort of choices and decisions we make in life, what sort of people we are going to be and what sort of way we are going to live. Faced with a decision that is a clear-cut choice between good and evil, it is easy to know what is the right one to make, even if we choose not to make it. More often than not, we are confronted with decisions where the choice is not between clearly perceived good or evil but between two or more options, all of which are possible choices. Sometimes we agonise over decisions because we are scared that we will make the wrong choice. To choose one thing is to reject another, and often part of us simply wants to sit on the fence, to have our cake and also to eat it.

Following Christ is not like that. He challenges us to make decisions and sitting on the fence is not an option. The Christian life involves decisions and choices; it involves taking risks in order to discover who we truly are and find our own true identity in God. Morris West writes:

> It costs so much to be a full human being that there are very few who have the enlightenment, or the courage, to pay the price ... One has to abandon altogether the search for security, and reach out to the risk of living with both arms. One has to embrace the world like a lover and yet demand no easy return of love. One has to accept pain as a condition of existence. One has to court doubt and darkness as the cost of knowing. One needs a will stubborn in conflict, but apt always to the total acceptance of every consequence of living and dying.[2]

Session 4

➲ **Introduction**   **(5–10 min.)**
Give each person a chance to share any thoughts about the last session or their week.

◀ **DVD**   **(9 min.)**
From where it finished last time (49.48) to 'He wasn't in the slightest bit judgemental about me or what I'd done. He took it very well' (58.26).

📖 **Read**   **(1 min.)**
Joe: 'You've got to make decisions. You've got to keep making decisions even if they're the wrong decisions. If you don't make decisions you're stuffed … and I really struggled to make that decision and I was so scared of going deeper.'

🗪 **Discuss**   **(5–10 min.)**
What do you think about what Joe said about making decisions?

📖 **Read**   **(3 min.)**
Joe: 'I was brought up a devout Catholic. I'd long since stopped believing in God. I'd always wondered, if things really hit the fan, I would, under pressure, turn around and say a few Hail Marys

and say, "Get me out of here." It never once occurred to me.'

Matthew 26:36–46: Jesus prays in Gethsemane.

🐾 **Discuss** **(5–10 min.)**
Does belief in God help in decision making or does it take away the need for decision making?

◀ **DVD** **(7 min.)**
From where it finished last time (58.26) to 'I think I knew the big picture of what was happening to me, and what I had to do was so big, I couldn't deal with it' (1:05.12).

📖 **& Read** **(1 min.)**
Joe: 'There's just no way you're physically going to do that. And then it occurred to me that maybe I should set definite targets. I started to look at things and think, right, if I can get to that crevasse over there in 20 minutes, that's what I'm going to do ... I think I knew the big picture of what was happening to me, and what I had to do was so big, I couldn't deal with it.'

🐾 **Discuss** **(5–10 min.)**
What do you think of Joe's approach to what he had to do?

📖 **Read** **(5 min.)**

Simon: 'There were all sorts of thoughts swirling around in my mind – guilt, worry, thinking about how on earth am I going to explain this to Joe's parents, my friends, to Richard? The thought did cross my mind that maybe I could think of a decent story that would make me look better and I did think about this for quite a while.'

Richard: 'I knew that they were both dead but I couldn't just clear off and leave the camp. For one thing, I didn't know anything about them except their first names, Joe and Simon. I didn't know their family names, and I had this bizarre idea that if they'd fallen off the mountain, and they would have just landed at the bottom of it, and I thought perhaps that from the bottom of the glacier I would be able to see them, and set off with the aim of going as far as I could.'

Simon, in *Touching the Void*: It was warm sitting on the hillock. Without realising I was doing it I told Richard exactly what had happened. I could have done nothing else. He sat silently listening to all that I had been through, not once questioning me, not looking surprised at what I was saying to him. I was glad I was telling him the truth. Not to have done so might have saved my hurt, but I knew as I told him that there was so much more we had managed to do that should be told. The rescue in the storm, the way we had worked together, the way we fought to get down alive. I couldn't say Joe had fallen into a crevasse when stupidly walking unroped on the glacier, not after he had been through so much trying to survive. I couldn't do him the injustice of lying, and my feeling of having failed him made it an impossibility to lie. When I had finished Richard looked at me: "I knew something terrible had happened. I'm just glad you managed to get down."'[3]

Discuss (5–10 min.)
What made Simon decide not to lie? What is Richard's role in the situation?

Ponder (1 min.)
Has there been a Richard figure in your life?

Share (5–10 min.)
Share your thoughts with the group or keep them to yourself if you'd rather.

Plan (2 min.)
Choose four readers from the group to read the parts of Joe, Simon and Richard and the Bible passages in next week's meditation.

Closing worship (5 min.)
See page 86.

On the Descent

'He sat silently listening to all that I had been through, not once questioning me, not looking surprised at what I was saying to him. I was glad I was telling him the truth.'

In some ways Richard has only a small part in the story but in another way he is very significant. When we looked at him in the first session, it was in the context of the story of the road to Emmaus; he was the stranger who joined the other two on their journey. At the end of this session he is there as the silent listener who doesn't pass judgement. In both instances we can choose to see him as a Christ figure – the one who joins them on the way and the one who does not judge.

In John's Gospel there is a passage (not found in the earliest manuscripts) which contains the story of the woman caught in the act of adultery (John 7:53-8:11). Significantly, it precedes a verse in which Jesus proclaims that he judges (or condemns) no one (8:15), a sentiment expressed elsewhere in John's Gospel (3:17; 12:47).

You can almost feel the glee of the teachers of the law and the Pharisees as they bring the woman into the temple courts and make her stand before the group that is listening to Jesus' teaching: 'Teacher, this woman was caught in the act of adultery. In the law Moses commanded us to stone such women. Now what do you say?' And then the Gospel writer adds: 'They were using this question as a trap, in order to have a basis for accusing him.'

The trap was similar to a question Jesus was asked on another occasion about paying taxes to Caesar (Mark 12:13-17) and is to do with the clash between Roman law and Jewish law. Under the Roman occupation it was not lawful for the Jews to put a person to death (as we see in the exchange between the crowd and Pilate in the passion narrative), but stoning was the punishment for adultery according to the law of Moses. If Jesus advocates stoning the woman, they can report him to the Roman authorities; and if he is lenient, they can denounce him as a blasphemer and breaker of the sacred law.

What does Jesus do? The Gospel writer continues: 'But Jesus bent down and started to write on the ground with his finger.' What did Jesus write? We have no idea, but that is not important. What matters is how he wrote, not what he wrote. He wrote on the ground with his finger, in the same way that the Ten Commandments had been written on tablets of stone by the finger of God (Exod. 31:18). In both instances it is the finger of God that is writing. And it is the finger of God that writes the law. The symbolism is plain: if you want to live by the law, then judge yourselves by the law, not just this woman. If you want justice, then want it for yourselves as well. 'Do not judge, or you too will be judged' (Matt. 7:1).

And one by one the accusers walked away, till only the woman and Jesus were left.

'Where are they?' asked Jesus. 'Has no one condemned you?'

'No one,' she said.

'Then neither do I,' replied Jesus. 'Go and sin no more.'

It's a strange thing that acceptance is a more powerful agent for change than judgement, though often we may think it's the other way round. These were the dying words of Anthony de Mello, a twentieth-century Jesuit priest, psychotherapist and spiritual writer:

> Don't change: Desire to change is the enemy
>   of love.
> Don't change yourselves: Love yourselves as
>   you are.
> Don't change others: Love others as they are.
> Don't change the world: It is in God's hands,
>   and he knows.
> And if you do that ... change will occur
>   marvellously in its own way and in its own
>   time.[4]

Week Five:

Out of the Void

On the Ascent

Visiting the places that Jesus visited has always been a part of the Christian tradition of pilgrimage. If you have ever travelled to the Holy Land, you may have visited the Chapel of the Ascension, located at the highest point in Jerusalem on top of the Mount of Olives. The present chapel is of Crusader origin, though it has been a site of pilgrimage since the fourth century AD. In the centre of the chapel is a stone with a foot-shaped mark worn within it. It is a mark that has been revered for centuries as the footprint of Christ, though countless pilgrims over the years have also left their own mark on the now rather worn old stone! A religious legend maybe, but nonetheless, a deeply symbolic one.

'Following in the footsteps of Jesus' is a phrase that is often used by tour companies offering pilgrimages to the Holy Land. Thinking about those footsteps, have you ever considered how far Jesus actually walked in his life? Walking was his only means of transport and, from what we read in the Gospels, he was always on the move.

We read that during his three-year ministry 'Jesus went about all the cities and villages teaching in their synagogues and preaching the gospel of the kingdom' (Matt. 9:35). Some of these cities and villages were 50, 60 or 70 miles away from his base in Capernaum. If you look at a map of the Holy Land, you can trace his journeys to places mentioned in the Gospels, such as Cana, Nain, Tyre and Sidon, Caesarea Philippi, Jericho and Bethany and the region of the Decapolis.

Jesus was always going somewhere. No wonder we read that 'foxes have holes and birds have their nests but the Son of Man has nowhere to lay his head'. A common estimate is that Jesus would have easily walked well over a thousand miles a year during his ministry. A lot of footsteps, and we are left with just one footprint! For centuries the Chapel of the Ascension has stood as a place of pilgrimage, as a symbolic reminder not only to all who are able to visit it, but also to Christians everywhere, that Jesus calls us to follow in his footsteps.

But you don't have to travel abroad to do this. The phrase 'following in the footsteps of Jesus' is also used to describe the life of Christian discipleship, and it means to walk the way that Jesus walked, to live our lives the way he lived his. It is therefore very appropriate that, according to Christian tradition, the last mark that Jesus left on earth before his ascension was a footprint, a sign that his way is also our way.

O let me see thy foot-marks,
And in them plant mine own;
My hope to follow duly
Is in thy strength alone:
O guide me, call me, draw me,
Uphold me to the end;
And then in heaven receive me,
My Saviour and my friend.[1]

Session 5

Introduction   (5 min.)
Ask if anyone wants to share any thoughts about
the last session or their week.

DVD   (6 min.)
From where it finished last time (1:05.12) to the
view of the lake after 'Get the remnants of the
mountain out of my system, really' (1:11.21).

Read   (2 min.)
Joe: 'I stayed on Simon's tracks and they were
weaving around over humps and past obvious
crevasses and stuff. I thought, well, unless I come
to a hole with his body in the bottom of it, these

tracks will lead me through the minefield of crevasses ...

'I could see Simon's tracks were filling in. They were my lifeline in the glacier and I started to get very desperate ...

'I carried on crawling in the dark. It was a stupid thing to do but I was frightened and I was just trying to see Simon's tracks ...

'In the morning it was a bright, sunny day. All the tracks had gone. I started quite early and every now and again I had to stand up on one leg to look around to try to see the way, then sit down again and shuffle along.'

Discuss   (10 min.)

Can you identify with Joe's situation? For example:

- What are the advantages and disadvantages of following footsteps?
- Have there been times when you have travelled in the dark?
- Where do you look to find your bearings?

DVD   (20 min.)

Fast forward to the view of the mountain at night (1:19.2) and play the film to the end. Let the music play and the credits roll for a while to give people space for thought.

✱ **Meditation** **(12 min.)**
The readers chosen last week now read the meditation
below, which uses extracts from the film together with
extracts from the Gospels:

Joe: 'The rest of that afternoon I was plagued by
this dreadful feeling that they would have gone.'

Matthew 26:40–41: He came back to the disciples
and found them sleeping, and he said to Peter, 'So
you had not the strength to stay awake with me
for one hour? Stay awake and pray not to be put
to the test. The spirit is willing enough, but
human nature is weak'.

Joe: 'I listened intently hoping to hear a whistle
or an answer, a cry back or something, and I
didn't hear anything at all. And I spent a long
time sat there crying, really not sure what to do,
and I thought about getting into my sleeping bag,
but for some reason it just seemed a bit of a
pathetic way to end things, just in a sleeping bag.'

Matthew 26:42: Again, a second time, he went
away and prayed: 'My Father,' he said, 'if this cup
cannot pass by, but I must drink it, your will be
done'.

Joe: 'As I was shouting, I thought this is it. This is

as far as this game goes. I'm not capable of going any further. I'd made the mistake of having a little bit of hope that they would still be there. And when I shouted and they weren't there I sort of knew that I was dead then.'

Matthew 26:45–46: Then he came back to the disciples and said to them, 'You can sleep on now and have your rest. Look, the hour has come when the Son of man is to be betrayed into the hands of sinners. Get up! Let us go! Look, my betrayer is not far away.'

Simon: 'I didn't want to leave immediately. I felt I needed a day or two just to collect my thoughts and to regain some strength. I spent a long time washing myself. That felt quite good – to wash my hair and to wash my face and to have a shave. To sort of get the remnants of the mountain out of my system, really.'

Matthew 27:24: Then Pilate saw that he was making no impression, that in fact a riot was imminent. So he took some water, washed his hands in front of the crowd and said, 'I am innocent of this man's blood.'

Joe: 'It was just a slow, steady reduction, not just physically but you, everything, yourself, and I felt left with nothing really … You just became almost nothing. It was strange.'

Matthew 27:33–40: When they had reached a place called Golgotha, that is, the place of the skull, they gave him wine to drink mixed with gall, which he tasted but refused to drink. When they had finished crucifying him they shared out his clothing casting lots, and then sat down and stayed there keeping guard over him. Above his head was placed the charge against him; it read: 'This is Jesus, the King of the Jews.' Then two bandits were crucified with him, one on the right and one on the left. The passers-by jeered at him; they shook their heads and said, 'So you would destroy the Temple and in three days rebuild it! Then save yourself if you are God's son and come down from the cross!'

Joe: 'That moment when no one answered the call – it was a loss of me. I lost me.'

Matthew 27:45–50: From the sixth hour there was darkness over all the land until the ninth hour. And about the ninth hour, Jesus cried out in a loud voice, 'Eli, eli, lama sabachthani?' that is, 'My God, my God, why have you forsaken me?' When some of those who stood there heard this, they said, 'The man is calling on Elijah,' and one of them quickly ran to get a sponge which he filled with vinegar and putting it on a reed, gave it him to drink. But the rest of them said, 'Wait! And see if Elijah will come to save him.' But Jesus, again crying out in a loud voice, yielded up his spirit.

Richard: 'I woke up not knowing why and was aware of this strange atmosphere. I could hear the wind howling outside the tent and started hearing something. It did slowly dawn on me that really the only thing it could be was Joe outside shouting but that was completely impossible because he was dead and he'd died three or four days ago. And then I heard it again much sharper and it really sounded like someone shouting, "Simon". I kind of got in a panic that first it couldn't be Joe because Joe's dead and then if he is out there it's going to be this horrible thing. It can't be a human being because no human being can possibly go through that and be outside the tent.'

Matthew 28:2–4: And suddenly there was a violent earthquake, for an angel of the Lord, descending from heaven, came and rolled away the stone and sat on it. His face was like lightning, his robe white as snow. The guards were so shaken by fear of him that they were like dead men.

Simon: '"Simon." It was quite clearly the shout of my name. I knew it was Joe actually. I knew immediately.'

John 20:11–16: But Mary was standing outside near the tomb, weeping. Then, as she wept, she stooped to look inside, and saw two angels in white sitting where the body of Jesus had been, one at the head, the other at the feet. They said, 'Woman, why are you weeping?' 'They have taken my Lord away,' she replied, 'and I don't know where they have put him.' As she said this she turned round and saw Jesus standing there, though she did not realise that it was Jesus. Jesus said to her, 'Woman, why are you weeping? Who are you looking for?' Supposing him to be the gardener, she said, 'Sir, if you have taken him away, tell me where you have put him, and I will go and remove him.' Jesus said, 'Mary!' She turned round then and said to him in Hebrew, 'Rabbuni!' – which means Master.

Simon: 'I couldn't completely believe it until I actually saw him, but then it was still a little difficult to believe that, because of the eerie night and the fact of the state he was in, an absolutely awful state. It was almost like he was a ghost-like figure. It was like I had to pinch myself almost to believe that this was true, that this was really happening.'

John 20:19–20, 24–25: In the evening of that same day, the first day of the week, the doors were closed in the room where the disciples were, for fear of the Jews. Jesus came and stood among them. He said to them, 'Peace be with you,' and after saying this, he showed them his hands and his side. The disciples were filled with joy at see-ing the Lord .... Thomas, called the Twin, who was one of the Twelve, was not with them when Jesus came. So the other disciples said to him, 'We have seen the Lord,' but he answered, 'Unless I can put my hand into his side, I refuse to believe.'

Simon: 'He thanked me for trying to get him down the mountain. For all that I'd done up to the point where I'd cut the rope. And he said to me, "I'd have done the same." Those were the first words he uttered.'

John 20:27–28: Then he spoke to Thomas, 'Put your finger here; look, here are my hands. Give me your hand; put it into my side. Do not be unbelieving any more but believe.' Thomas replied, 'My Lord and my God!'

Richard: 'And I remember that before we had done anything to him, before we had even closed the door, he said, "Where are my trousers?" We had to explain that we had burnt his trousers, which made him quite angry. And I think that kind of brought me back into life to some extent, realising that it was the same old Joe back again.'

Luke 24:33–35, 52: There they found the Eleven assembled together with their companions, who said to them, 'The Lord has indeed risen and has appeared to Simon.' Then they told their story of what had happened on the road and how they had recognised him at the breaking of bread .... They worshipped him and them went back to Jerusalem full of joy ....

( ) Conclusion   **(30 min.)**
Each person in turn briefly shares their thoughts about the course.

☼ Closing worship   **(5 min.)**
See page 86.

On the Descent

For many, if not most, of the people following this course as a Lent Course, next week will be what the Church calls Holy Week. The Church calls just one week 'Holy', a reminder of how special that week is. The services of Holy Week provide the opportunity for us to enter into the last days of Jesus' journey and help us to see that his journey is also our journey, his story is also our story. We too can make holy our experiences of love and friendship, loss and pain.

And that has been the purpose of this course, made more explicit in the meditation that ended this last session. Interspersing extracts from the passion narrative with the film narrative makes the point that our faith is about making sense of our own journey through life in the light of Jesus' journey on earth. And it was, of course, with the theme of life being a journey that we began this course.

Many churches dramatise the reading of the passion on Palm Sunday in some way. The symbolism enables us to understand that we are not simply listening to a story but are witnessing a dramatic event in which we all play our part. And perhaps, without us even realising it, we already have our part written for us in the character of Barabbas. He was the prisoner Pilate chose to release instead of Jesus at the request of the crowd, and his name may well have a special significance.

Bar means 'son of' in Aramaic and is found in a number of biblical names, including Bartimaeus, son of Timaeus (Mark 10:45), and Simon Bar-Jona, son of Jona (Matt. 16:17). *Abba* means 'father' in Aramaic (Mark 14:36), so *Barabbas* literally means 'son of the father', which basically means everyone. To modern readers the masculine language might make this sound non-inclusive, but it is actually the most inclusive name possible – we are all sons (or daughters) of a father.

Barabbas is every man or, more accurately, Everyman. He represents us all. Jesus died in order that Barabbas could go free, just as he died in our place so that we may go free. 'Were you there when they crucified my Lord?' asks the American spiritual. Well, yes, you were. We are all Barabbas.

But not only were we there, so that Jesus' story is also our story; he is also here and our story is also his story. Just as we can find ourselves within the passion narrative, in his story, we can find Jesus in our story. Deborah Jones writes:

> When we begin to share the story of our lives with others, when we open up to our brothers and sisters, we can be helped to see how God is working in our lives. To hear the story of another's life and experience is to receive a precious gift. It is to discover an unwritten page of Scripture.[2]

Take time to reflect on the stories you have heard told by your fellow travellers and the story you have told them. They are a precious gift.

> You yourselves are our letter, written in our hearts, that everyone can read and understand, and it is plain that you are a letter from Christ,

entrusted to our care, written not with ink, but
with the Spirit of the living God; not on stone
tablets but on the tablets of human hearts.

2 Corinthians 3:2–3

Closing
Worship

Closing
Worship

Leader: Let us pray.

A short silence is kept.

Leader: O God, for your love for us, warm and
           brooding,
           which has brought us to birth and opened
           our eyes
           to the wonder and beauty of creation.

All: We give you thanks.

Leader: For your love for us, wild and freeing,
           which has awakened us to the energy of
           creation:
           to the sap that flows, the blood that pulses,
           the heart that sings.

All: We give you thanks.

Leader: For your love for us, compassionate and
           patient,
           which has carried us through our pain,

wept beside us in our sin,
and waited for us in our confusion.

All: We give you thanks.

Leader: For your love for us, strong and challenging,
which has called us to risk for you,
asked for the best in us and shown us how
    to serve.

All: We give you thanks.

Leader: O God, we celebrate that your Holy Spirit is
    present
deep within us and at the heart of life.
Forgive us when we forget your gift of love
made known to us in Jesus, and draw us
    into your presence.

Sharing
*The leader invites people to share a brief thought or picture
from the session which struck them in some way. Thoughts
are simply aired and no comments on them are made by
others.*

Leader: O Trinity of Love:
        You have been with us at the world's
          beginning.

All: Be with us till the world's end.

Leader: O Trinity of Love:
              You have been with us at our life's shaping.

All: Be with us at our life's end.

Leader: O Trinity of Love:
              You have been with us at the sun's rising.

All: Be with us till the day's end. Amen.

Leader: May God, who is present in sunrise and
                  nightfall,
              in the crossing of the sea
              and on the high mountain,
              guide our feet as we go.
              May God, who is with us when we sit
              and when we stand,
              encompass us with love
              and lead us by the hand.
              May God, who knows our path
              and the places where we rest,
              be with us in our waiting,
              be in us at our sharing
              and go with us at our ending.

All: Amen.
              Adapted from *The Iona Abbey Worship Book*
              (Wild Goose Publications, 2001)

Leaders' Notes

The course
The five sessions are designed to run from the week after Ash Wednesday until the week before Holy Week. There is no need for people to have seen the film beforehand. The story is easy to follow and virtually all the film is seen during the sessions.

Traveller's diary
People should be encouraged to keep a journal or 'Traveller's Diary'. These can be simple exercise books, or a set for the group can be easily made by folding five A4 sheets into an A5 booklet and stapling it in the middle, to give a cover page and two A5 pages for each session. A personal record of thoughts in a diary/journal is a helpful addition to the course for some people, and in the first two sessions there is time given over to making personal notes.

The group
A group of not more than ten people is best, though the sessions will work with a small group of four or five as well.

The leader

Each session needs to have a group leader. The leader requires no special knowledge, but needs to be familiar with the session beforehand. He or she does need to be able to lead the group discussions, ensuring that everyone has a chance to speak if they would like to and that no one is allowed to dominate the discussion.

Course structure

Each group session is preceded by a section called 'On the Ascent' and followed by one called 'On the Descent'. These are designed to give additional food for thought to the course as a whole and do not figure directly in the group sessions. They are to be read individually by group members in their own time.

The suggested timings of the group sessions should be followed as closely as possible to give a session length of 90 minutes. It is best to be fairly strict about timing as it will enable the session to flow, but at times sensitivity to something that is being said will mean that the timings may need to be interpreted with some flexibility.

The structure of the group sessions

◀ DVD

The leader needs to be familiar with when each clip begins and ends, and should set up the first clip before the session begins. Some groups may have a video of the film, so should refer to the video timings on p. 93.

📖 Read

Passages are either printed in the group session notes or taken from the Bible. At least one Bible needs to be available to read from at each session, though group members can have individual copies if they wish. The passages should be read out loud by group members chosen in turn by the leader. The leader needs to be sensitive to the fact that not everybody likes reading out loud and should check beforehand.

💬 Ponder

This gives people a minute or two to think in silence about the question and how it relates to their own life. It is very important that this time of silence is taken and it is the leader's job to make sure it happens.

💬 Share

Throughout the sessions the phrase 'Share your thoughts with the group or keep them to yourself if you'd rather' occurs under this heading. This is an essential point and needs to be respected by everyone in the group. Listen if people choose to share, but do not push people if they choose not to. Nobody should ever be made to feel that they should say something if they don't want to.

🗨 Discuss

The subjects under this heading are of a less personal and more general nature and do not have a pause for thought ('Ponder') before them. All the questions are deliberately open, so different groups are likely to respond to them in different ways. There are no right or wrong answers!

ᑌᕈ Personal reflection
This heading occurs in the first two sessions where people are asked to write down some of some of their own thoughts. This is a way of introducing the concept of the journal/diary. The leader will need to make sure people have something to write in and with, particularly in these sessions, but also in the others, as group members may like to jot down some of their thoughts and impressions.

☼ Closing worship
Each session ends with a short act of worship which can be found on p. 86. This includes a time of silence during which the leader invites people to share a thought or picture from the session which struck them in some way. It is very important that these are simply put into the silence and no comment is made on them by others. It is not a time of discussion. The leader only needs to acknowledge each contribution with a simple 'thank you'. If nobody says anything, the silence is just held for a couple of minutes.

Video References

Week 1

◀ **Video** (7 min.)

From VCI logo (1.04) to just after when Joe says, 'Christ it's big. Looks harder than I thought, expected. But I was excited' (8.00).

◀ **Video** (8 min.)

From end of last clip (8.00) to '... it was going to go tits up, so we dug a snow cave' (15.15).

Week 2

◀ **Video** (7 min.)

From where it finished last time (15.15) to 'that night as we made a brew the gas ran out' (21.56).

◀ **Video** (17 min.)

From where it finished last time (21.56) to 'And I would have died pretty soon actually. The wind chill was very low' (38.40).

Week 3

◀ **Video** (3 min.)

From where it finished last time (38.40) to 'I could smell the water in the snow around me. I felt it very strongly. It was quite a strange thing' (41.32).

◀ **Video** (8 min.)

From where it finished last time (41.32) to 'I just cried

and cried. I thought I'd be tougher than that' (48.58).
Note: this extract contains strong language.

◀ **Video** **(2 min.)**

From where it finished last time (48.58) to 'an
absolutely enormous crevasse 30 feet wide and bottomless from where I was looking at it' (51.00).

Week 4

◀ **Video** **(9 min.)**

From where it finished last time (51.00) to 'He wasn't
in the slightest bit judgmental about me or what I'd
done. He took it very well' (59.40).

◀ **Video** **(7 min.)**

From where it finished last time (59.40) to 'I think I
knew the big picture of what was happening to me
and what I had to do was so big I couldn't deal with
it' (1hr 06.24).

Week 5

◀ **Video** **(6 min.)**

From where it finished last time (1hr 06.24) to the
view of the lake after 'Get the remnants of the mountain out of my system, really' (1hr 12.37).

◀ **Video** **(20 min.)**

Fast forward to the view of the mountain at night (1hr
20.20) and play the film to the end. Let the music play
and all credits role. Don't stop until the music stops.

Notes and References

The Scripture quotations in this publication are taken from the New Jerusalem Bible, published and copyright 1966, 1967 and 1969 by Darton, Longman and Todd and Doubleday and Co. Inc.

Unless otherwise stated, all quotes are from the film *Touching the Void*, based on the book of the same name by Joe Simpson, directed by Kevin Macdonald © Film 4 and the UK Film Council, 2003, in association with Channel 4 and PBS, a Darlow Smithson Film and Television production.

Introduction
1. Joe Simpson, *This Game of Ghosts* (Vintage, 1994).
2. Simon Yates, *The Flame of Adventure* (Vintage, 2002).
3. Sebastian Faulks, *Engleby* (Vintage, 2008).
4. Joe Simpson on www.noordinaryjoe.co.uk
5. Simon Yates, *The Flame of Adventure* (Vintage, 2002).
6. Joe Simpson, *The Beckoning Silence* (Vintage, 2003).
7. Rodgers and Hammerstein, in *The Sound of Music* (1959).

Week One: Travelling Companions
1. See an example at http://pictureswithamessage.com/78/cat78.htm?931
2. Joe Simpson, *Touching the Void* (Vintage, 1997).
3. Margaret Silf, *At Sea with God* (Darton, Longman and Todd, 2003).

4. C. S. Lewis, *The Lion, the Witch and the Wardrobe* (Collins, 2001).
5. Prayer of St Francis of Assisi (1182–1226).

Week Two: Plateaux and Summits

1. Simon Yates, *The Flame of Adventure* (Vintage, 2002).

Week Three: Breaking Free

1. *Common Worship: Services and Prayers for the Church of England* © The Archbishops' Council 2000.
2. *The Book of Common Prayer* (Cambridge University Press).
3. Simon Yates, *Against the Wall* (Vintage, 1998).
4. Joe Simpson, *Touching the Void* (Vintage, 1997).
5. Simon Yates, *Against the Wall* (Vintage, 1998).
6. C. S. Lewis, *The Silver Chair* (Collins, 2000).

Week Four: Decision Making

1. For more on this idea and the background to it, see David Gibson: http://www.beginningwithmoses.org/briefings/luke4v1to13.htm
2. Morris West, *The Shoes of the Fisherman* (The Toby Press, 2003), quoted in John Powell, *Why Am I Afraid to Tell You Who I Am?* (Fontana/Collins 1983).
3. Joe Simpson, *Touching the Void* (Vintage, 1997).
4. Anthony de Mello is quoted in Carlos Valles, *Mastering Sadhana* (Fount, 1988).

Week Five: Out of the Void

1. 'O Jesus I have promised', words by John Ernest Bode, 1868.
2. Deborah Jones, *Focus on Faith: a resource for the journey into the Catholic Church* (Kevin Mayhew, 1996).